Grade

➤ APPENDIX

Paths to College and Career

English Language Arts

Protocols, Strategies, and Graphic Organizers

PCG | Education

JOSSEY-BASS™
A Wiley Brand

Cover design by Wiley

Published by Jossey-Bass
A Wiley Brand
One Montgomery Street, Suite 1000, San Francisco, CA 94104-4594—www.josseybass.com

Jossey-Bass books and products are available through most bookstores. To contact Jossey-Bass directly call our Customer Care Department within the U.S. at 800-956-7739, outside the U.S. at 317-572-3986, or fax 317-572-4002.

Wiley publishes in a variety of print and electronic formats and by print-on-demand. Some material included with standard print versions of this book may not be included in e-books or in print-on-demand. If this book refers to media such as a CD or DVD that is not included in the version you purchased, you may download this material at http://booksupport.wiley.com. For more information about Wiley products, visit www.wiley.com.

ISBN: 978-1-119-15511-9

Printed in the United States of America

FIRST EDITION

PB Printing 10 9 8 7 6 5 4 3 2 1

CONTENTS

Introduction

This book includes all protocols referenced in the *Paths to College and Career* modules for grades 6–8. It also includes descriptions of a host of strategies used in the lessons in those modules, related to checking for understanding, ongoing assessment, and building academic vocabulary. There are also valuable resources related to the modules, such as information on helping students read closely and annotate text, and a section of reproducible graphic organizers.

PROTOCOLS

Entrance and Exit Tickets

Purpose

At the end of class, students write on note cards or slips of paper an important idea they learned, a question they have, a prediction about what will come next, or a thought about the lesson for the day. Alternatively, students turn in such a response at the start of the next day—one based on the learning from either the day before or the previous night's homework. These Quick Writes can be used to assess students' knowledge or to make decisions about next teaching steps or points that need clarifying. This reflection helps students focus as they enter the classroom or solidifies learning before they leave.

Procedure

- For 2–3 minutes at the end of class (or at the start of the next one), have students jot responses to the reading or lesson on 3-by-5 note cards.
- Keep the response options simple—for example, "Jot down one thing you learned and one question you have."
- A variation is known as 3-2-1: Have students write three of something, two of something, then one of something. For example, students might explain three things they learned, two areas in which they are confused, and one thing about which they'd like to know more or one way the topic can be applied. The criteria for listing items depend on your needs and those of the lesson, but it's important to make the category for three items easier than the category for listing one item.
- Don't let the cards become a grading burden. Glance over them for a quick assessment and to help you with planning for next learning needs. These are simple Quick Writes, not final drafts.
- After studying the "deck," you might pick out a few typical, unique, or thought-provoking cards to spark discussion.
- Consider typing up cards (perhaps keeping them anonymous) to share with the whole group to help with summarizing, synthesizing, or looking for important ideas. It is a good idea to let students know ahead of time that you will be doing this, as they may put more effort into the write-up. When typing, go ahead and edit for spelling and grammar.

Back-to-Back and Face-to-Face

Purpose

This protocol provides a method for sharing information and gaining multiple perspectives on a topic.

Procedure

These instructions are for the student.

1. Find a partner and stand back-to-back with him or her. Be respectful of space.
2. Wait for the question or opinion that you will be asked to share with your partner.
3. Think about what it is you want to share and how you might best express yourself.
4. When the facilitator says, "Face-to-face," turn, face your partner, and decide who will share first if the facilitator has not indicated that a certain person should go first.
5. Listen carefully when your partner is speaking and be sure to give him or her eye contact.
6. When given the signal, find a new partner, stand back-to-back, and wait for your new question or opinion.
7. This may be repeated for as many rounds as needed or appropriate.

Building Background Knowledge

Purpose

This protocol demonstrates how quickly people can become interested in a topic, build background knowledge, and use that background knowledge to become better and more informed readers of complex text. The protocol adapts easily to content in many disciplines, and the design ensures that all participants read, think, and contribute. The protocol is particularly useful in introducing a topic because it fosters curiosity and builds in immediate feedback about learning. When conducted and debriefed for educators, the protocol heightens awareness of key instructional and grouping practices.

Procedure

1. Choose a topic and find text as described in the next steps.
2. Group participants: Use a grouping strategy to shift participants into groups of four or five.
3. Distribute materials: for each group, a set of four different colored markers, a piece of chart paper, texts, and loose-leaf paper.

4. Share a "mystery text": Choose a relevant short text, poem, political cartoon, photograph, song, graph, map, and so on that sparks participants' curiosity about the topic. Display or provide copies of the text (remove the title if it gives away the topic).
5. Have participants write down what they think the mystery text is about, and draw a line after thoughts are jotted down.
6. Activate and share background knowledge:
    - Ask participants to write what they know about the topic in their journals.
    - Ask participants, in their small groups, to share what they know about the topic.
    - Ask participants to create a web or visualization of their collective knowledge/understanding of the topic on a piece of chart paper using just one of the colored markers.
7. Provide a "common text"—an article or essay on the topic that is interesting, offers a solid introduction to the topic, and provides multiple perspectives. All participants read this article.
8. Ask participants to text-code the article with "N" for new information.
9. Ask participants to add their new knowledge to their web using a different color of marker.
10. Distribute "expert texts": Hand out a different text on the topic to each member of the group.
11. Again, ask participants to text-code for new information, using the third color.
12. After everyone has read, each participant shares new knowledge with his or her group and captures key points on the chart paper using the fourth color.
13. Have on hand extra texts or additional media (drawings, maps, photos, graphs, and so on) for those who finish early.
14. Return to the mystery text. Reread/display the initial text again.
15. Ask participants to go back to where they had initially written about the mystery text; have participants note what they now think about the mystery text.
16. Debrief the experience:
    - Contrast the first and second reading/showing of the mystery text: "What was it like to hear the mystery text the second time?" "What made the experience so different?"
    - Ask a general question about what the process of reading successive articles was like. Did they know much about the topic before? Had they been curious about the topic? What inspired their curiosity?

Carousel Brainstorm

Purpose

The purpose of using the Carousel Brainstorm protocol is to allow participants to share their ideas and build a common vision or vocabulary; facilitators can use this process to assess group knowledge or readiness around a variety of issues.

Procedure

1. Before the class gathers, identify several questions or issues related to your topic, perhaps drawn from a reading that you will share later.
2. Post your questions or issues on poster paper.
3. Divide the class into smaller teams to match the number of questions you have created.
4. Distribute materials: for each group, a different colored marker and loose-leaf paper.
5. Have each team start at a particular question.
6. At each question, participants should brainstorm responses or points they want to make about the posted question.
7. After the teams have spent a couple of minutes on a question, signal the teams to move to the next question, until all teams have responded to all questions.
8. You can conclude the activity by having each team highlight key points to discuss with the class.
9. If it is appropriate for your topic, distribute a related reading and discuss, using the common vocabulary you have built through this process.

Chalk Talk

Purpose

A Chalk Talk is a way to promote discussion and awareness of issues and perspectives—silently. A Chalk Talk is also an excellent way to promote awareness of patterns and problems and to ensure that all voices are heard.

Procedure

1. Formulate an important, open-ended question that will provoke comments and responses.
2. Provide plenty of chart paper and colored pencils and arrange a good space for participants to write and respond. Write the question or topic in the middle of the paper in bold marker.
3. Explain the Chalk Talk protocol and answer any participant questions.
4. Establish rules for the Chalk Talk. This technique works only if everyone is writing and responding throughout the designated time period. Make it clear that everyone is responsible for writing, reading other people's comments, and responding; there should be no talking, and no one should sit down until the time period is over. Opinions must be freely expressed and honored, and no personal attacks are allowed.
5. Allow 10–20 minutes for the Chalk Talk. As facilitator, it's helpful to walk around and read, and gently point participants to interesting comments. All writing and responding is done in silence.

6. Search for patterns. In pairs, participants should read through all the postings and search for patterns and themes (or "notice and wonder"). This part takes about 5 minutes.
7. Conduct a whole-group share. Pairs should report out patterns and themes, round-robin style, until all perceptions are shared.
8. Debrief the process. What was the experience like of "talking" silently?

Concentric Circles (Inner Circle/Outer Circle)

Purpose

This protocol provides participants with a structure to actively engage in discussions around short text, questions, opinions, or debates on any topic with several different partners.

Procedure

1. Arrange desks or chairs in two concentric circles facing each other.
2. The first pair of students facing each other will have a specified amount of time to discuss the first question, topic, or section of a reading.
3. When the signal is given, the inside circle rotates one chair (or more) to the right or left, and the new pair moves on to the next question, topic, or section of reading.
4. The inside circle moves as many times as necessary to finish the topics.
5. The last pair should have time to sum up the conversation and be prepared to share key points with the whole group.
6. Debrief: Share important ideas or common threads to the discussions as appropriate.

Variations: Participants could define terms or prep for tests. The protocol could be used to role-play or critique.

Discussion Appointments

Purpose

Discussion Appointments allow students to have conversations with various peers about a text, question, or concept. Multiple short discussions allow students to expand and deepen their understanding. For this reason, the Discussion Appointments protocol is particularly good to use just before students begin to write.

Procedure

1. Determine the focus of the discussions. Have clear questions or prompts to provide to students.
2. Determine the number and length of appointments students will have.
3. Create an appointments sheet, or create a model for students to replicate.
4. Explain to students the purpose and logistics of the Discussion Appointments, and distribute (or have them create) their appointments sheet.
5. Give students a brief amount of time (usually about 3 minutes) to set appointments, having them write down the name of their "appointment." Students should have only one appointment per slot, and they may not turn down an invitation for an appointment if both people have the same open slot.
6. If there is an uneven number of students, or if students do not have an appointment slot filled for some other reason, they should come to you to be paired up or to engage in discussion with you.

Final Word

Purpose

This protocol is designed to help participants understand the meaning of a text, particularly to see how meaning can be constructed and supported by the ideas of others. After the presenter shares his or her thinking, interesting similarities and differences in interpretations will arise as other participants share their thinking without judgment or debate. The presenter listens and may then change his or her perspective, add to it, or stick with original ideas without criticism. This protocol is especially helpful when people struggle to understand their reading.

Procedure

1. Have each group select a time keeper and facilitator.
2. All participants may read the same text, or participants may read different texts on a common topic for a Jigsaw effect. Text selection is a critical step.
3. Participants read silently and text-code or fill out a recording form based on desired outcomes. They clearly mark passages for discussion so that they can quickly locate them later. To promote critical thinking, design the discussion prompts such that they ask participants to include their reasons for selecting a particular passage and to provide evidence that supports a particular point.
4. Presenter shares a designated number of passages and his or her thinking about them.
5. In less than 1 minute, each participant comments on what was shared.

6. Presenter gets the "final word," sharing how his or her thinking evolved after listening to others, or reemphasizing what was originally shared.
7. Follow steps 4–6 with each additional participant taking the role of presenter.
8. Debrief the content. Presenters discuss how hearing from others affected their thinking.
9. Debrief the process. What worked in our discussion? What were some challenges? How can we improve next time?

Fishbowl

Purpose

The fishbowl is a peer-learning strategy in which some participants are in an outer circle and one or more are in the center. In all fishbowl activities, both those in the inner and those in the outer circle have roles to fulfill. Those in the center model a particular practice or strategy. Participants in the outer circle act as observers and may assess the interaction of the center group. Fishbowls can be used to assess comprehension, assess group work, encourage constructive peer assessment, discuss issues in the classroom, or model specific techniques, such as literature circles or Socratic Seminars.

Procedure

1. Arrange chairs in the classroom in two concentric circles. The inner circle may be only a small group or even a pair.
2. Explain the activity to the students and ensure that they understand the roles they will play.
3. You may either inform in advance those who will be on the inside, so they can be prepared, or just tell them as the activity begins.
4. The group in the inner circle interacts using a discussion protocol or script.
5. Those in the outer circle are silent, and are given a list of specific actions to observe and note.
    - One idea is to have each student in the outer circle observing one student in the inner circle. (You may have to double, triple, or quadruple up.) For example, students in the outer circle can tally how many times their "assigned" student participates or asks a question.
    - Another way is to give each student in the outer circle a list of aspects of group interaction that they should observe and comment on—for example, whether the group members take turns, use names to address each other, or let everyone's voice be heard.
6. Make sure all students have turns being in the inside and the outside circles at some point, although they don't all have to be in both every time you do a fishbowl activity.

7. Debrief: Have inner-circle members share how it felt to be inside. Outer-circle members should respectfully share observations and insights. Discuss how the fishbowl could improve all group interactions and discussions.

Variation: Each person in the outside circle can have one opportunity during the fishbowl to freeze or stop the inside participants. This person can then ask a question or share an insight.

Gallery Walk/Hosted Gallery Walk

Purpose

This protocol offers participants an opportunity to share information with others in a gallery setting. The protocol involves small-group collaboration, while making individuals responsible for the learning and, when hosted, the teaching.

Procedure

1. Divide participants into groups—the size of the group will vary with the topic and how it can be divided, the size of the class, the age of participants, and so on.
2. Assign each group a specific segment of the topic (for example, the legislative branch of government, the role of a worker bee, or transportation on the river).
3. Provide each group with additional materials they need to further enhance the study that has already been introduced, probably in a large-group setting (for example, government, insects, importance of the river).
4. Allow time for the group to read and discuss the new information. Have each group use prior knowledge along with the new knowledge to create a chart with key points and a visual representation that—in the hosted version—each person in the group will use to teach others in the class.
5. Be clear that each person has to understand the text and images on the poster in order to present the information effectively. Allow time for the group members to help one another focus on key components.
6. Post the work around the room or in the hallway.
7. Regroup participants so that each new group has at least one member from the previously established groups.
8. Give specific directions indicating the poster at which each group will start and what the rotation will look like.
9. The speaker at each poster is the person(s) who participated in the creation of the poster.

10. When all groups have visited each poster, debrief. Possible debrief questions:
    - What was your biggest "aha" during the tour?
    - How was your learning enhanced by this method?
    - What role did collaboration play in your success?
    - Why was the individual responsibility component so important?

Give One, Get One, Move On (GoGoMo)

Purpose

This is a protocol that can follow any workshop, exploration, research, or experience. Use it to spread good ideas and to see what "stuck" with participants. You can structure it with movement or make it a silent, written experience.

Procedure

1. Ask participants to write down three to five key learnings or important ideas about the topic of study. You may choose to have people write each idea on a different index card or sticky note to give away to his or her partners.
2. Invite the group to get up and mingle with their peers or colleagues.
3. After about 30 seconds, call out "give one to a partner."
4. Participants form pairs and each "gives" one of his or her key learnings or important ideas about the topic to the other, so each person "gives one" and "gets one." Time may range from 1–3 minutes.
5. Call out "move on," and participants mingle again.
6. Repeat the sharing for as many ideas as people have to share.

Variations

- For sharing, vary the sizes of the groups from pairs to triads to quads.
- Instead of random mingling, have people gather in various clusters, such as by height, by interest, by role, and the like. This slightly changes the focus of sharing.
- See a silent, written version described in the next section.

Give One, Get One, Move On (GoGoMo)—Written Version

Procedure

1. Provide each student with a copy of the chart shown here.
2. Have students think of an important idea they have learned about this topic or one that has recently been reinforced. Ask them to write it down in box 1 on their chart.
3. Ask students to pass the sheet to another participant who will silently read what the first student has written in box 1. That person will add an idea in box 2. No one should repeat ideas that are already listed.
4. Students continue passing on the paper and adding ideas until all the boxes are filled with ideas. Return the sheet to the original owner.

1	2	3
4	5	6
7	8	9

Infer the Topic

Purpose

This protocol offers students a chance to work together to uncover the heart of a larger concept before they begin to study a new topic. Students also get a chance to experience the ways an inference can change as they take in new information. It allows students to draw on their own background knowledge and work with new information from a variety of peers to uncover meaning in a fun, collaborative environment.

Procedure

1. Locate artifacts with and without key words/quotes related to the concept. The goal is for students to infer what is happening in the image. Images can range from concrete to abstract.
2. Have students select an image and record their inference about the new topic of study.
3. Students mingle about the room and stop when prompted, facing a partner.
4. In 1 minute or less, students view each other's images, then discuss and record a new inference about the upcoming topic of study.
5. Students mingle about the room again, this time with the partner they were just sharing with. When prompted, partners stop, facing another set of partners.
6. All four students share their artifacts and inferences, discuss further, and make a new inference about what the new topic of study could be.
7. Students gather as a whole group, displaying their artifact in front of them for all to see. The teacher invites a few to share their artifacts and their inferences about the upcoming topic.
8. After a few have shared, the teacher reveals the topic of study as well as the guiding questions and big ideas.
9. Debrief: Ask students to share a final inference about the meaning of their images and how they relate to the larger concept(s). Discuss how students' inferences did or didn't change throughout this protocol. Ask students to name strategies for inferring and to ask lingering questions about the topic. Also, discuss what it was like to engage this way. Consider recording debrief notes on an anchor chart.

Variations

- Vary partner instructions or adapt numbers of partners or rounds.
- To monitor understanding and support students struggling to infer the artifacts' meaning, you can circulate and give these students a "ticket" in the form of a colored card or sticky note. At an opportune time, call a meeting of an invitational group for anyone with tickets or anyone who is struggling.

Interactive Word Wall

Purpose

An Interactive Word Wall in a classroom is a powerful instructional tool to strengthen content vocabulary. It is an organized collection of words (and sometimes phrases) displayed on a wall or other space in the classroom. Consider writing both academic and discipline-specific words on large index cards, strips of paper, or tag board so that they can be easily manipulated. For English Language Learners and young learners, it could be helpful to place an illustration, photograph, or object on or next to particular words to support students' learning through the aid of visual cues.

Procedure

Multiple Ways to Interact with Words

The "interactive" part is critical; actively engaging with the words will support student learning. There are many ways to interact with word walls; some interactions are quick and can occur on a daily basis. Other interactions can constitute an entire lesson. The following are some suggestions:

Categorize and classify: Have students classify the terms.

Compare and contrast: Create categories to compare and contrast.

Draw a map: Use the words to create a concept map.

Illustrate a model: Use the words to construct a conceptual model that represents student thinking and/or a scientific phenomenon.

Create descriptions: Use the words to describe concepts.

Contextualize use: Challenge the students to use some or all of the words on a short-answer quiz.

Label diagrams: Use the words on the wall to label student diagrams and illustrations.

Concept Map Approach

One of the most common approaches to interacting with words on a word wall is to use the concept map, which provides students with an opportunity to demonstrate and enhance their understanding of a related set of terms:

1. Pull cards from your word wall, or write one word/phrase per card. Use a limited number of cards, perhaps 10–15, or fewer for younger students.
2. Also create cards with one-way and two-way arrows. Use the floor or magnets and a magnetic board to display the cards, and group the students around the words. (Modification: Give each student his or her own set of word cards.)
3. Ask a student or a pair of students to arrange two or three cards in a way that connects them or makes a model of the terms.

4. Ask the student(s) to explain what they are doing as they place the words.
5. Observers may ask questions once the connection or model is created.
6. Repeat with another student or pair of students.
7. Debrief. Possible debrief questions:
    - How did working with the cards help you better understand the topic?
    - How was your thinking similar to or different from the student doing the arranging?
    - Are there words you would add or subtract?

Jigsaw

Purpose

This protocol allows small groups to engage in an effective, time-efficient comprehension of a longer text. Having every participant read every page or section may not be necessary. Participants can divide up the text, become an expert in one section, hear oral summaries of the others, and still gain an understanding of the material.

Procedure

1. Divide the chosen text into manageable sections.
2. Arrange participants into groups so that there are the same number of people in each group as there are sections to read. Assign a section to each student.
3. Participants read their section independently, looking for key points, new information, or answers to questions.
4. Each member in turn shares his or her important points or summaries of the text.
5. Have participants independently write and reflect on their own understanding after the discussion.
6. Debrief: Have groups or individuals share insights and discoveries. Did the group process help members gain an understanding of the whole text? What worked well for the group? Are there discussion skills the group could improve? Are there any lingering questions or misconceptions about the topic?

Example

Reading Assignments

Reader 1: pages 62–64 (The Mouth)

Reader 2: page 65 (The Esophagus)

Reader 3: page 66 (The Stomach)

Reader 4: pages 67–68 (The Small Intestine)

After reading, readers get together in topic-alike ("expert") groups (all the Reader 1s, Reader 2s, and so on) to compare notes and ideas. They determine importance, discuss the main idea(s), and develop a clear summary to share with others.

Then, participants gather in their Jigsaw groups (Readers 1, 2, 3, and 4) to share their notes and summaries. Jigsaw groups are given a task that requires the application of all pieces of information gathered from each expert.

Mystery Quotes

Purpose

This protocol offers participants a chance to work together to uncover the heart of the meaning of a mystery quote, passage, or image before they read more about it or work more deeply with inference as a critical thinking strategy. It allows participants to work in a fun, collaborative environment to use new information from a partner and to draw on their own background knowledge to uncover meaning. This protocol also asks participants to put things in their own words, compare text to experience, and work with a variety of partners.

Procedure

1. Decide on quotes, phrases, sentences, or words directly from the text to copy onto strips or index cards.
2. Don't paraphrase the text. You may omit words to shorten a sentence, but don't change the words.
3. Have participants select a quote/passage and, without revealing it to his or her partner, tape it on the partner's back. Participants may look for a partner who seems like just the right person for the quote, or selections can be randomly determined.
4. Participants mingle about the room and stop when prompted, facing a partner.
5. In 1 minute or less, participants read each other's quotes and think about one hint to give the partner about his or her quote.
6. In 1 minute total, each participant shares a hint about the partner's quote.
7. Participants mingle about the room again and stop when prompted, facing another partner.
8. Offer time for students to read the quote and think about a story that exemplifies or reminds them of it.
9. Each participant shares the story related to the partner's quote in a set time frame.
10. Continue additional rounds as desired, offering a range of prompts right for your situation, such as "Create a metaphor or simile to describe the quote" or "Give an example of the idea in the quote in action."

11. Debrief: Bring the whole group together for each participant to share a final inference about the meaning of each quote. Participants then pick their quotes from a list of all quotes. For more support, participants can pick their quotes first and share how their inferences compare to the actual text. Discuss strategies for inferring, respond to lingering questions about the activity, and discuss what it was like to engage this way. Consider recording debrief notes on an anchor chart.

Variations

- Participants carry index cards with them, recording their current thinking about the essence of their quotes after each partner activity.
- Vary partner instructions or adapt numbers of partners or rounds.
- To monitor understanding and support participants struggling to infer their quote's meaning, you can circulate and give these participants a "ticket" in the form of a colored card or sticky note. At an opportune time, call a meeting of an invitational group for anyone with tickets or anyone who is struggling.
- For nonreaders, use images with or without key words. The goal is to infer what is happening in the image on your back. Images can range from concrete to abstract. It is also possible to divide the class into readiness groups and have one group work separately with sentences while the other uses images.

Peer Critique

Purpose

This protocol can be used to offer critique and feedback in preparation for revision of work. It should be used after the completion of a draft of what will become a finished product. This process will help participants see what is working and then ask questions and offer suggestions, leading to revision and improvement. It is important that participants understand that the focus should be on offering feedback that is beneficial to the author/creator. Explicit modeling is necessary for this protocol to be used successfully.

Procedure

1. Begin with the non-negotiables:
   - **Be kind:** Always treat others with dignity and respect. This means we never use words that are hurtful, including sarcasm.
   - **Be specific:** Focus on particular strengths and weaknesses, rather than making general comments like "It's good" or "I like it." Provide insight into why it is good or what, specifically, you like about it.

- **Be helpful:** The goal is to positively contribute to the individual or the group, not to simply be heard. Echoing the thoughts of others or cleverly pointing out details that are irrelevant wastes time.
- **Participate:** Peer critique is a process to support each other, and your feedback is valued!

2. Have the author/designer explain his or her work and explain exactly what type of critique would be helpful—in other words, what questions he or she has or what he or she is confused about that he or she would appreciate help with.
3. The critique audience should begin comments by focusing on something positive about the work ("warm" feedback), then move on to constructive sharing of issues or suggestions ("cool" feedback).
4. When critiquing a peer's work, students should use "I" statements—for example, "I'm confused by this part," rather than "This part makes no sense." Remember the three important phrases:
   - "I notice . . ."
   - "I wonder . . ."
   - "If this were my work, I would . . ."
5. Students should use questions whenever possible—for example, "I'm curious why you chose to begin with . . .?", or "Did you consider adding . . .?"

Popcorn Read

Purpose

A Popcorn Read helps a group determine importance and synthesize their understanding of a text.

Procedure

1. Select a piece of text. Consider your purpose when choosing your text. Have participants highlight information that stands out to them in the text. (You may want to give them the criteria first, so they know what length of phrase they're looking for.)
2. Post and discuss the criteria for a good-spirit read ahead of time:
   - Read short phrases or words only (not sentences).
   - Give no commentary or opinions.
   - Try to connect with what was just read (listen carefully to others).
   - Give all voices a chance.
   - Pauses can be powerful.
   - Repeating phrases is OK (shows where a group collectively agrees).

3. Have the group form a circle. One person starts the group off by reading a word or phrase; the other participants search for a phrase they've underlined that matches or connects in some way with the phrase just heard. This process continues until there are no more phrases people want to share aloud (until there are no more "kernels left to pop").
4. Debrief afterward:
   - How did underlining key points help you better understand the text?
   - How did it help to hear what others read aloud?
   - What was it like to try to connect words and phrases?

Praise-Question-Suggest

Purpose

This protocol can be used to offer critique and feedback in preparation for revision of work. It should be used after the completion of a draft of what will become a finished product. This process will help participants see what is working and then ask questions and offer suggestions, leading to revision and improvement. It is important that participants understand that the focus should be on offering feedback that is beneficial to the author/creator. Explicit modeling is necessary for this protocol to be used successfully.

Procedure

1. Provide product descriptors and rubrics as clear guidelines of the expectations and criteria for the piece of work that will be critiqued. If the work is written, copies for the critique group are helpful.
2. As a whole group, create or refer to a list of revision questions based on the criteria for the piece of work.
3. Model the procedure with the whole group before allowing small independent feedback groups.
4. Participants work in groups of two to five.
5. The first participant presents/reads the draft of her piece. She may ask peers to focus on a particular listed revision question or two that she is struggling with.
6. Feedback is best written on sticky notes and given to the creator. Peers first focus on what is praiseworthy or working well. Praise needs to be specific. Simply saying, "This is good" doesn't help the creator. Comments such as "I notice that you used descriptive picture captions" or "You have a catchy title that makes me want to read your piece" are much more useful.
7. Next, peers ask questions and offer helpful suggestions. "This part is unclear. I wonder if it would be better to change the order of the steps?" or "I can't tell the setting. Maybe you could add some details that would show the reader where it is taking place?" or "I wonder if adding a graph to highlight your data would be effective?"
8. Feedback should relate to the revision questions identified by the group or presenter.

9. After each member of the group has offered feedback, the presenter discusses which suggestions she wants to implement and thanks the group.
10. Others then present their work in turn and cycle through the feedback process.

Quiz-Quiz-Trade

Purpose

Quiz-Quiz-Trade is a vocabulary reinforcement protocol that both allows students to review key vocabulary terms and definitions from their reading and gets them moving and interacting with peers.

Procedure

1. Choose 15–20 high-frequency academic and/or domain-specific words from class reading(s). (*Note:* You may want to list a word more than once or twice if it is essential to students' understanding of text and/or used more frequently than other words in common texts.)
2. Create vocabulary "strips" with these words, folded vertically so one side of the slip shows the word, and the other side of the slip has the definition.
3. Give each student one vocabulary strip.
4. Each student finds a partner.
5. Partner A shows the side of the paper with the word on it to his or her partner.
6. Partner B says the definition (if he or she knows it), or finds the word in the text and tries to determine the definition, using context clues.
7. Partner A then reads the definition aloud to confirm or correct the definition that Partner B gave.
8. Partners switch roles and repeat the preceding steps.
9. Partners then trade vocabulary slips and find a new partner.
10. Students should meet with at least two or more partners during this activity (5–10 minutes).
11. After completing the preceding steps, gather students as a whole group. Make sure to review and emphasize vocabulary that you want students to know and understand, as individual students will not have had the opportunity to see and define every key term during this activity.

Sample Vocabulary Strips

foliage	Plant life
marvelous	Amazing; spectacular; wonderful
ascent	Climb; move upward

sort	Place into categories; arrange; classify
specimens	Examples; samples; a type of something

Rank-Talk-Write

Purpose

This protocol, adapted from "Pause, Star, Rank" in Himmele and Himmele (2011), allows participants to actively review their notes about new concepts as well as analyze and discuss the importance of key ideas they identify.

Procedure

1. During or after reading a text, participants independently write a summary sentence for each key idea or concept they identify.
2. Participants then rank the summary sentences in order of importance (1 next to most important, 2 and 3 next to the second and third most important summaries of each concept.)
3. In groups, participants share out the concepts they ranked, explaining why they ranked each concept as they did in terms of importance.
4. Each group determines which one concept they think is most important, and discusses the best summary statement for that idea or concept.
5. A scribe from the group writes the summary statement of the idea or concept on a whiteboard, piece of chart paper, or large blank page.
6. Small groups share their idea summary statement with the large group.

Reference

Himmele, Pérsida, and William Himmele. *Total Participation Techniques: Making Every Student an Active Learner.* Alexandria, VA: ASCD, 2011.

Say Something

Purpose

Say Something is a paired reading strategy developed by Egawa and Harste (2001) for constructing meaning from text-based information. Through structured exchanges, group members develop relationships between new information and what they already know or believe. This thinking out loud, supported by attentive listening, enhances individual and shared understandings. The time frame for this strategy is intentionally brief. It is effective to post a public timer displaying the full time allotment so that partners can determine how long to converse and how quickly to move on to the next reading.

Procedure

1. Identify the text and the stopping points, or have partners look over a piece of text and decide together how far they will read silently before stopping to *say something.*
2. Describe the nature of the interactions, explaining that the "something" might be a question, a brief summary, a key point, an interesting idea, or a new connection. (To focus the paired interactions or to stimulate a specific type of thinking, you may want to provide a stem for completion. For example, "A question that comes to mind when I read this is . . ." Use the same stem for each stopping point, or provide variation.)
3. Model. Provide one or two examples of appropriate *say somethings.* These should be succinct, thoughtful, and related to the text.
4. Have participants begin reading the text.
5. Once each partner has reached the chosen stopping point, both partners exchange comments, or *say something.*
6. Partners continue the process until the selection is completed.
7. After a designated amount of time, engage the whole group in a discussion of the text.

Reference

Egawa, Kathryn, and Jerome C. Harste. "Balancing the Literacy Curriculum: A New Vision." *School Talk* 7, no. 1 (2001).

Science Talks

Purpose

Science Talks are discussions about big questions. They are appropriate for any grade level, but they are particularly useful for elementary school. Like a Socratic Seminar, Science Talks deal with provocative questions, often posed by students themselves. Science Talks provide space for students to collectively theorize, build on each other's ideas, work out inchoate thoughts, and learn about scientific discourse. Most important, they allow all students to do exactly what scientists do: think about, wonder about, and talk about how things work, the origins of phenomena, and the essence of things. Your task during a Science Talk is to listen very carefully and to follow student thinking. These talks provide a window on student thinking that can help you figure out what students really know and what their misconceptions are. Armed with this insight, you can better plan hands-on activities and experiments. Students become more motivated to do these activities because they are truly on a "need-to-know" basis.

Procedure

1. **Setting culture:** Science Talks are a valuable tool for working on the culture of the classroom, as well as for working on the social construction of meaning. Students sit in a circle and direct their comments to one another, not to you. In fact, you stay quiet and out of the way, facilitating only to make sure that students respectfully address one another and to point out when monopolizing behavior occurs. Students sense the importance of these talks, and appreciate having their thoughts and attempts at verbalizing valued. In a good talk, you'll hear students saying, "I want to add to what Grace said . . ." or "I think Derek is right about one thing, but I'm not so sure about . . ." These norms should be explicitly addressed before a Science Talk commences and debriefed at the end.
2. **Choosing the question:** The best questions are provocative and open-ended, so as to admit multiple answers and theories. Often, students generate great questions for Science Talks. To hear those questions, however, means that you must pay close attention to "kid talk" during science activities, while doing and debriefing field work, and other opportunities during the day. Often, the "Wonder" part of a K-W-L will include great wonderings that can't be answered with a simple fact. You can also generate questions based on your own wonderings. Often, as you think through and write the rationale and guiding questions for your expeditions, you will identify your own burning questions about a topic.
3. **Introducing Science Talks to students:** Gather students into a circle on the floor. Introduce the first Science Talk by discussing what scientists do. Students have theories about that, too. By saying that what we're about to do now is exactly what scientists do when they get together heightens the drama, value, and anticipation. Then ask, "What will help us talk as scientists?" Record the students' comments, as these will become the norms for your Science Talks. If the students don't mention making sure that everyone has a chance to talk, introduce that idea, as well as how each person can ensure that he or she doesn't monopolize the conversation. Stress how each student's voice is valued and integral to the success of a Science Talk. Another good question to pose is, "How will we know that what we've said has been heard?" Students will readily talk about how they can acknowledge what's been said by repeating it or rephrasing before they go on to add their comments. This is a great place to add (if the students don't) that talking together is one way that scientists build theories.
4. **Conducting the Science Talk:** With young students, it is often helpful to first do a movement exercise that relates to the Science Talk. For a talk on how plants grow, for example, students can be invited to show, with their bodies, how plants grow from bulbs. This gives students not only a chance to move before more sitting but also a different modality in which to express themselves. Sometimes the shyer students find that acting something out first helps them verbalize during the talk. It's helpful for you to record the talks, as it's hard to catch everyone's line of reasoning.

Replaying the tapes later helps make sense of what at first hearing can seem incomprehensible. Students also love hearing the tapes of Science Talks. A typical talk lasts about 30 minutes. It can be helpful for you to take notes during the talk as to who is doing the talking, and to record particularly intriguing comments.

5. **Debriefing the Science Talk:** The debrief should only take a couple of minutes, and it should refer to the norms and goals for the talk. Asking what they might work on next time will help students set a goal for the next talk.
6. **Planning follow-up activities and documenting student thinking:** It's very helpful to document student thinking expressed during a talk. There are several ways to do this. One way is to transcribe the talk and post it in the classroom. Figuring out experiments and hands-on activities that address students' questions and hypothetical answers are logical next steps.

Socratic Seminar

Purpose

Socratic Seminars promote thinking; meaning making; and the ability to debate, use evidence, and build on one another's thinking. When well-designed and implemented, the seminar provides an active role for every student, engages students in complex thinking about rich content, and teaches students discussion skills. One format for the seminar is as follows.

Procedure

1. Select a significant piece of text or a collection of short texts related to the current focus of study. This may be an excerpt from a book or an article from a magazine, journal, or newspaper. It might also be a poem, short story, or personal memoir. The text needs to be rich with possibilities for diverse points of view.
2. Develop an open-ended, provocative question as the starting point for the seminar discussion. The question should be worded to elicit differing perspectives and complex thinking. Participants may also generate questions to discuss.
3. Participants prepare for the seminar by reading the chosen piece of text in an active manner that helps them build background knowledge for participation in the discussion. The completion of the pre-seminar task is the participant's "ticket" to participate in the seminar. The pre-seminar assignment could easily incorporate work on reading strategies. For example, you might ask students to read the article in advance and to text-code by underlining important information and by putting questions marks next to segments they wonder about and exclamation points next to parts that surprise them.
4. Once the seminar begins, all participants should be involved and should make sure others in the group are drawn into the discussion.

5. Begin the discussion with the open-ended question designed to provoke inquiry and diverse perspectives. Inner-circle participants may choose to move to a different question if the group agrees (see "Option: Using a Fishbowl"), or you may pose follow-up questions.
6. The discussion proceeds until the you call time. At that time, the group debriefs their process; if using a fishbowl, the outer-circle members give their feedback sheets to the inner-group participants.
7. If using a fishbowl, you may allow participants in the outer circle to add comments or questions they thought of while the discussion was in progress.

Criteria

Participants . . .

- **Respect other participants.** They exhibit open-mindedness and value others' contributions.
- **Are active listeners.** They build on one another's ideas by referring to them when it is their turn to talk.
- **Stay focused on the topic.**
- **Make specific references to the text.** They use examples from the text to explain their point.
- **Give their input.** They make sure to participate.
- **Ask questions.** As needed, they ask clarifying questions to ensure that they understand the points others are trying to make, and ask probing questions that push the conversation further and deeper when appropriate.

Sample Checklist of Specific Look-Fors

Did the Participant . . .	Consistently	Occasionally	No	Notes/Comments
Respond to other participants' comments in a respectful way?				
Listen attentively without interruption?				
Use eye contact with peers?				

Exhibit preparation for the seminar?				
Reference the text to support his or her response?				
Participate in the discussion?				
Ask clarifying and/or probing questions?				

Option: Using a Fishbowl

When it is time for the seminar, divide participants into two groups if there are enough people to warrant using a fishbowl approach. One group forms the inner circle (the "fish") that will be discussing the text. The other group forms the outer circle that will give feedback on content, contributions, and/or group skills. (*Note:* Fishbowls may be used with other instructional practices, such as peer critiques, literature circles, or group work. If the number of participants in the seminar is small, a fishbowl does not need to be used.) Each person in the outer circle is asked to observe one of the participants in the inner circle. Criteria or a rubric for the observations should be developed by participants or shared with them in advance.

Take a Stand

Purpose

Participants articulate and reflect on their opinions about controversial questions.

Procedure

1. Post two signs at either end of an imaginary line that goes across the classroom. At one end of the line, post "Strongly Agree." At the other end, post "Strongly Disagree."
2. Tell participants that today they will be using the Take a Stand protocol, which will allow them to share and explain their opinions. After they hear a statement, they will move along the imaginary line to a place that best reflects their beliefs. (Note that you can have participants stand up or sit down in their places.)

3. Explain the steps of the protocol:
    a. The facilitator will make a statement and then participants will move, according to whether they agree or disagree with that statement, to a place on the imaginary line that goes across the room. Point out that one side of the room is labeled "Strongly Disagree" and the other side labeled "Strongly Agree," and this means that the middle of the line is undecided.
    b. After the facilitator makes a statement, he or she will pause for participants to think, and then ask all participants to move to the place on the imaginary line that best reflects their opinion.
    c. The facilitator will ask participants to share and justify their opinion, making sure to hear from people on different parts of the line.
    d. If a participant hears an opinion that changes his or her mind, the participant can move quietly to a different part of the line.
4. Model how the protocol will work. Make a statement (for example, "Chocolate ice cream is delicious") and show students how you would move to reflect your opinion. The modeling helps participants internalize how to use the invisible line.
5. As you use the protocol, repeat each statement twice.

Tea Party

Purpose

This protocol offers participants a chance to consider parts of the text before they actually read it. It encourages active participation and attentive listening while offering a chance to get up and move around the classroom. It allows participants to predict what they think will happen in the text as they make inferences, see causal relationships, compare and contrast, practice sequencing, and draw on prior knowledge.

Procedure

1. Decide on phrases, sentences, or words directly from the text to copy onto strips or index cards.
2. Don't paraphrase the text. You may omit words to shorten a sentence, but don't change the words.
3. Have students organized into groups of four or five.
4. Hand out the strips or cards with phrases from the text; two (or more) students will have the same phrases.
5. Each student independently reads his or her phrase and makes a prediction about what this article could be about. Then he or she writes a quick statement on a prediction recording form.
6. Next, students mingle around the room, reading to each other and discussing possible predictions.

7. Ask students to return to their small group and, as a group, write a prediction starting with "We think this article will be about . . ., because . . ." Have them also list questions they have.
8. Now, have students read the selection, independently or as a group, highlighting information that confirms or changes their predictions.
9. Ask students to write a statement on the second part of the recording form about their revised predictions. They should also continue to list lingering questions.
10. Debrief: Share out thoughts from groups. How did their predictions differ from the text? What lingering questions do they have? What was it like to engage in reading in this way?

Think-Pair-Share (Ink-Pair-Share; Write-Pair-Share)

Purpose

This protocol ensures that all participants simultaneously engage with a text or topic. It allows participants to recognize and speak their own ideas (or commit them to paper) before considering the ideas of others.

Procedure

1. Give students a short and specific time frame (1–2 minutes) to **think** or **ink** (write) freely to briefly process their understanding or opinion of a text selection, discussion question, or topic.
2. Ask students to share their thinking or writing with a peer for another short and specific time frame (for example, 1 minute each).
3. Lead a whole-class sharing of thoughts, often charting the diverse thinking and patterns in participant ideas. This helps both you and the students assess understanding and clarify ideas.

World Café

Purpose

A World Café is an opportunity to discuss a topic or various topics, rotating the role of leadership and mixing up a group of people.

Procedure

1. Have students form three groups of three or four and ask them to sit together at a table.
2. Each group selects a leader.
3. The leader's role is to record the major points of the conversation that takes place at the table and to then summarize the conversation using the recorded notes at the appointed time (see step 6).

4. The group discusses the topic at hand until time is called. Groups can be discussing the same topic or related topics.
5. The leader stays put; the rest of the group rotates to the next table.
6. The leader (the one who didn't move) presents a summary of the conversation recorded from the former group to the new group.
7. Each table selects a new leader.
8. Again, the new leader's role is to record the major points of the conversation that takes place at the table and to then summarize the conversation using the recorded notes at the appointed time (see step 11).
9. The group discusses the topic at hand until time is called.
10. Repeat the process, ideally until all participants have had a chance to lead.
11. After the final round, the last group of leaders presents to the whole group rather than reporting out to a "next rotation."

Written Conversation

Purpose

Created by Daniels and Zemelman (2004), Written Conversation harnesses the universal urge to share via written notes. After reading (or hearing a lecture, watching a video, or doing an experiment), pairs of students write short notes back and forth to each other about the experience. Think of Written Conversation as legalized note passing, taking the place of class discussion as a key after-reading activity. "Class discussion" can too often mean 1 person talking and 29 others sitting, pretending to listen. With Written Conversation, you can have a "discussion" in which everyone is actively talking at once—though silently and in writing.

Procedure

1. After the reading is completed, have students identify partners for a written conversation. If necessary, you can pair students.
2. Explain the activity first, if this protocol is new to them so that students understand that they will be writing simultaneous notes to each other about the reading selection, swapping them every 2–3 minutes at the teacher's command, for a total of three exchanges (or two or four, depending on your time constraints), and keeping quiet along the way. They are to write for the whole time allotted for each note, and put down words, phrases, questions, connections, ideas, wonderings—anything related to the passage or responding to what their partner has said, just as they would in an out-loud conversation. Spelling and grammar do not count—after all, these are just notes.

3. You can leave the topic open—for example, "What struck you about this reading?" Or give an appropriate open-ended prompt: "What do you understand and not understand in this selection?" "What are the most important ideas here?" "Do you agree or disagree with the author, and why?"
4. Both students in each pair start writing a note (for example, "Dear Bobby, When I read this chapter I was amazed that Abraham Lincoln actually said . . ."). Meanwhile, watch the time, and after 2–3 minutes, ask student to exchange notes. Remind students: "Read what your partner said, then take 2 minutes to answer just as if you were talking out loud. You can write responses, feelings, or stories; make connections of your own; or ask your partner questions—anything you would do in a face-to-face conversation."
5. After the planned two- to three-note exchange is complete, the payoff comes when you say: "OK, now you can talk out loud with your partner for a couple of minutes." You should notice a rising buzz in the room, showing that the students have plenty to talk about.
6. Next, a short whole-class discussion can be much more engaging and productive, because everyone will have fresh ideas about the topic. Ask a few pairs to share one highlight or thread of their written conversations as a way of starting the discussion.

Some predictable problems are likely to occur.

- The first time you try this, the students will tend to shift into oral conversation when papers are passed. (Adults also do this; it's a normal human response when you are bonding with a partner.) Be ready to remind them to "keep it in writing" during the transitions.
- Even with the best instructions, some kids will write two words and put their pens down, wasting 2 good minutes of writing time with each pass. You have to keep stressing, "We write for the whole time." If necessary, provide additional prompts to the class or individuals to help them keep going.
- After you call students back to order at the end, when they are talking out loud with their partners, you might find it hard to get them back. This happy little "management problem" shows you that students are connecting to each other and the materials.

Reference

Daniels, Harvey, and Steven Zemelman. *Subjects Matter: Every Teacher's Guide to Content-Area Reading.* Portsmouth, NH: Heinemann, 2004.

STRATEGIES

Checking for Understanding and Ongoing Assessment Strategies

When you check all students' levels of understanding throughout each lesson, you set the tone that everyone's thinking is important and necessary, and you forward the learning and engagement of all. Some techniques are too time consuming to use as quick pulse checks, but using these strategies in lessons allows you to track learning and adapt instruction appropriately on the spot.

Cold calling: Name a question before identifying students to answer it, and call on students regardless of whether they have hands raised. Call on students by pulling ***equity sticks*** or name cards, or by using a tracking chart to ensure that all students contribute. Scaffold questions from simple to increasingly complex, probing for deeper explanations. Connect thinking threads by returning to previous comments and connecting them to current ones; model this for students and teach them to do it too. In this way, listening to peers is valued, and even after a student has been called on, he or she is part of the continued conversation and class thinking.

Equity sticks: These are wooden sticks (tongue depressors, popsicle sticks, or craft sticks) with each student's name written on one stick. Equity sticks are often used for cold calling or forming random groups.

Fist-to-Five: To show degree of agreement, readiness for tasks, or comfort with a concept or learning target, students can quickly show their thinking by holding up (or placing near the opposite shoulder) a fist for zero/Disagree or one to five fingers for increasing levels of confidence or agreement.

Four Corners: Students form four groups (vary the number depending on the purpose) based on commonalities in their responses to a question posed. Once students physically move to a "corner" of the room based on their answer, they discuss their thinking, and one student from each group shares the group's ideas with the whole class. Students in other groups/corners may move to that corner if they change their thinking based on what they hear.

Glass-Bugs-Mud: After students try a task or review a learning target or assignment, they identify their understanding or readiness for application using the windshield metaphor for clear vision: glass = totally clear; bugs = a little fuzzy; mud = I can barely see.

Guided practice: After students have grappled with a challenging task, you can provide guided practice before releasing students to independent application. During guided practice, students quickly try the task at hand in pairs or in a low-stakes environment. You strategically circulate, monitoring students' readiness for the task and noting students who may need reteaching or who would benefit from an extension or more challenging independent application. Use an appropriate quick-check strategy to determine needs for differentiation during independent application time.

Hot Seat: Place key reflection or probing questions on random seats throughout the room. When prompted, students check their seat and answer the question. Students who do not have a Hot Seat question are asked to agree or disagree with the response and explain their thinking.

Human Bar Graph: Identify a range of levels of understanding or mastery (for example, beginning/developing/accomplished or Confused/I'm OK/I am rocking!) as labels for three to four adjacent lines. Students then form a human bar graph by standing in the line that best represents their current level of understanding.

Learning Line-Ups: Identify one end of the room with a descriptor such as "Novice" or "Beginning" and the other end as "Expert" or "Exemplary." Students place themselves on this continuum based on where they are with a learning target, skill, or task. Invite them to explain their thinking to the whole class or the people near them.

Milling to Music: Students share their thinking, class work, or homework in an interactive way with their peers. This activity is similar to Musical Chairs, except that there are no chairs and no one gets "tagged out." While the music is playing, students should dance around to move throughout the room; when the music stops, each student shares his or her thinking or work with the student closest to him or her. Have students do this twice, so that they have the opportunity to share with two peers.

No Opt Out: Require all students to correctly answer questions posed to them (in cases where questions have a "correct" answer). Follow incorrect or partial answers until a correct answer is given by another student, either through cold calling or asking for a volunteer. Then, return to any student who gave an incorrect or partial answer and have him or her give a complete and correct response.

Presentation quizzes: When peers present, ensure that other students know they are responsible for learning the information by pairing student presentations with short quizzes at the end of class.

Red Light, Green Light: Students have red, yellow, and green objects accessible (for example, popsicle sticks, poker chips, or cards), and when prompted to reflect on a learning target or readiness for a task, they place on their desk the color that describes their comfort level or readiness (red = stuck or not ready; yellow = need support soon; green = ready to start). Target your support for the reds first, then move to yellows and greens. Students change their colors as needed to describe their status.

Release and Catch/7:2: When students are working on their own, they often need clarification or pointers so that they do not struggle for too long a period or lose focus. A useful ratio of work time to checks for understanding or clarifying information is 7 minutes of work time (release), followed by 2 minutes of teacher-directed clarifications or use of a quick-check strategy (catch).

Sticky Bars: Create a chart that describes levels of understanding, progress, or mastery. Have students write their names or use an identifying symbol on a sticky note and place their notes on the appropriate place on the chart.

Table Tags: In three areas of the room, place paper signs or table tents with colors, symbols, or descriptors that indicate possible student levels of understanding or readiness for a task or target. Students sit in the area that best describes them, moving to a new area when relevant.

Thumb-ometer (and other "-ometers"): To show degree of agreement, readiness for tasks, or comfort with a learning target or concept, students can quickly show their thinking by putting their thumb up, to the side, or down. Feel free to get creative with other versions of "-ometers" that allow students to physically demonstrate where they are with a target or concept.

Tracking Progress: Post a chart on the wall and/or distribute individual charts displaying learning targets and levels of proficiency. Students indicate their self-assessed level of proficiency, usually multiple times. Students can use different colored dots, ink stamps, or markers and/or dates to indicate progress over time.

Turn and Talk: When prompted, students turn to a shoulder buddy or neighbor and, in a set amount of time, share their ideas about a prompt or question posed by you or other students. Depending on the goals of the lesson and the nature of the Turn and Talk, students may share some key ideas from their paired discussions with the whole class.

Whip-Around (Go-Around): When a brief answer can show understanding, self-assessment, or readiness for a task, ask students to respond to a standard prompt one at a time, in rapid succession around the room.

Whiteboards: Students have small whiteboards at their desks or tables and write down their ideas/thinking/answers and hold up their boards for scanning by you or their peers.

Strategies for Building Academic Vocabulary

Components of Vocabulary Instruction

Introduce and activate word meanings:

- Present words in a variety of contexts.
- Provide multiple opportunities to learn and expand on meanings.
- Promote active and generative processing.
- Provide ongoing assessment and communication of progress.

Guidelines for Selecting Vocabulary

Do . . .	Avoid . . .
Teach fewer vocabulary terms, but teach them in a manner that results in deep understanding of each term. Less is more—depth is more.	Teaching or assigning words from textbooks just because they are highlighted in some way (italicized, in bold face, and so on).
Teach terms that are central to the unit or theme of study. These are terms that are so important that if the student does not understand them, he or she is likely to have difficulty understanding the remainder of the unit.	Teaching or assigning words just because they appear in a list at the end of a text chapter.
Teach terms that address key concepts or ideas. Although a text chapter may contain 15–20 vocabulary terms, there may be only four or five—and sometimes only one or two!—that address critical concepts in the chapter.	Teaching or assigning words that will have little utility once the student has passed the test.

Teach terms that will be used repeatedly throughout the semester. These are foundational concepts on which a great deal of information will be built over the long term.	Assigning words that you cannot define.
	Assigning large quantities of words.
	Assigning words that students will rarely encounter again.

Contextual Redefinition

Contextual Redefinition offers students specific steps for deducing the meaning of unknown (or unclear) words in a reading passage by seeking clues from the words' context in a larger text selection. This strategy encourages students:

- To focus on what is clear and obvious in a reading selection
- To state, as much as is possible, the author's general intent/meaning in a passage
- To use these observations to help interpret unclear terms and ideas within the known context

In addition, Contextual Redefinition calls for close attention to word order, syntax, parallel ideas, and examples as keys for predicting word meaning.

Steps to Contextual Redefinition

1. Select several key words from a reading selection (especially words that have multiple meanings or might otherwise be unclear to readers). Write these words on the chalkboard.
2. Have students suggest definitions for these terms before reading the selection. Most likely, students will provide a range of definitions, because they are considering the words in isolation from any specific context. Some of the proposed definitions will be inexact, hinting at but not fully defining, the term.
3. Record on the chalkboard all definitions suggested.
4. Have the students read the text selection, noting the specific sentences in which each of the words appears.
5. Ask students to revisit their previous definitions and see which, if any, reflect the use of these words in the context of the selection. Use dictionaries if student definitions lack enough clarity to match the contextual meaning of the words.
6. Reiterate that words have multiple meanings and uses and that the context of a word in a text selection determines its meaning.

Learn More

Lenski, Susan D., Mary Ann Wham, and Jerry L. Johns. *Reading and Learning Strategies for Middle and High School Students.* Dubuque, IA: Kendall/Hunt, 1999.

Elaboration Techniques

There are several Elaboration Techniques that appear to be particularly powerful facilitators of comprehension and memory of new terms. These are briefly described in the next sections.

Elaboration Technique 1

Teach new terms in the context of a meaningful subject-matter lesson, and facilitate student discussion that centers on use of the new term. At some point, students should use the new term themselves in a sentence within the context of discussing broader topics. The traditional practice of having students look up definitions and then write sentences using the new terms likely stems from the idea that students must think of the term and create a context for which it might be appropriately used. Although composing written sentences is clearly an important elaboration technique for the learner, learning about the term within an overall context is also essential so that the student can develop relational understanding.

Although providing opportunities for students to elaborate on new terms requires a significant portion of class time, it is clearly a worthwhile instructional practice. The problem is, students are often expected to memorize the definitions of far more terms than there is time in class to elaborate on. To provide meaningful opportunities for elaboration, you need to teach considerably fewer terms and invest considerably more time in developing deep knowledge structures for those that are truly essential for students to know. The adage "less is more—depth is more" is very true in this case.

Elaboration Technique 2

Facilitate paraphrasing of a new term's definition so that students can identify the core idea associated with the overall meaning of the term, as well as distinguish the new term's critical features. If you were to dissect the semantic structure of a new term, you would find that its definition actually has two main components: (1) the core idea of the new term, which is like its "gist" or main idea; and (2) critical features of the definition that clarify the broader, more general core idea. This is analogous to paraphrasing main ideas of paragraphs when reading, whereby the reader states what the overall paragraph was about (main idea) and indicates important details in the paragraph. With new terms, the goal is to paraphrase the core idea of the term and identify specific critical-to-remember details that clarify the core idea.

Elaboration Technique 3

Make connections between background knowledge and the new term. Although teaching the new term in the context of a subject-matter lesson is a critical instructional technique, an equally important elaboration technique is for students to relate the term to something with which they are already familiar. There is a wide array of methods by which students can formulate knowledge connections. For example, they can identify how the term is related to subject matter they have learned previously; they can identify something from their personal life experiences that the term reminds them of; they can create metaphors or similes for the term; or they can say how the term relates to understanding or solving a real-life problem. An essential part of this elaboration process is having the students explain the connection. For example, a student should not only state what personal experience the term makes him or her think of but also explain why that experience reminds him or her of the term.

Elaboration Technique 4

Identify examples/applications as well as nonexamples/nonapplications related to the new term's meaning. Comprehension is greatly enhanced if the learner can accurately identify examples of the term or ways the new term can be appropriately applied within the context of discussing another subject. For example, the term *peaceful resistance* might be used when describing Martin Luther King's approach to solving racial discrimination problems.

You will likely find that students' comprehension of new terms becomes considerably more focused and refined if students can also identify examples of what the term is not about or examples of inappropriate applications of the term's use. Having the students discuss what the term is not an example of, or identify another concept with which someone should not confuse the term, can facilitate this kind of learning.

Elaboration Technique 5

Create multiple formats through which students can elaborate on the meaning of new terms. Many teachers will use all the aforementioned elaboration processes within the context of a class discussion, yet some students will still not seem to "get it." This is because the ways in which elaboration was facilitated were all "lip-ear"—verbal or listening—forms of instruction. Written elaborations, even for those students for whom scripting is a laborious process, creates an opportunity for greater reflection on the term's meaning. Other forms of elaboration involve role playing the meanings of some terms or creating mnemonic pictures or stories that capture the essence of a new term's meaning.

The Clarifying Routine focuses on ways each of the previously described forms of elaboration can be facilitated. In this routine, you use an instructional tool, called a Clarifying Table, to facilitate these kinds of thinking behaviors. The accompanying graphic illustrates a Clarifying Table that was used in the context of an integrated unit with a *Titanic* theme.

CLARIFYING TABLE

Term
Elitism

Core Idea
being especially proud of belonging to a small group who thinks it's superior

☑ Use it to describe . . . ☐ Use it to describe . . .	Clarifiers	Knowledge Connections
how many 1st class passengers behaved on the Titanic	* "superior to other" belief * "more valuable" belief	snobby-acting movie stars
	* snobby acting * member of aristocracy	banker's wife on Beverly *Hillbillies*
☑ Don't confuse it with . . . ☐ Not an example of . . . empathy—sensing and caring how others feel when they have problems	* usually the super-rich, celebrities, and stars	The Yacht Club

Example Sentence
Elitism occurs when you act like you are more special than everybody else.

Frayer Model

The Frayer Model is a graphic organizer used for word analysis and vocabulary building. This four-square model prompts students to think about and describe the meaning of a word or concept by

1. Defining the term
2. Describing its essential characteristics
3. Providing examples of the idea
4. Offering nonexamples of the idea

This strategy stresses understanding words within the larger context of a reading selection by requiring students, first, to analyze the items (definition and characteristics) and, second, to synthesize and apply this information by thinking of examples and nonexamples.

Steps to Using the Frayer Model

1. Explain the Frayer Model graphic organizer to the class. Use a common word to demonstrate the various components of the form. Model the type and quality of desired answers when giving this example.
2. Select a list of key concepts from a reading selection. Write this list on the chalkboard and review it with the class before students read the selection.

3. Divide the class into student pairs. Assign each pair one of the key concepts and have them read the selection carefully to define this concept. Have the pairs complete the four-square organizer for their assigned concept.
4. Ask the student pairs to share their conclusions with the whole class. Use these presentations to review the entire list of key concepts.

Frayer Model

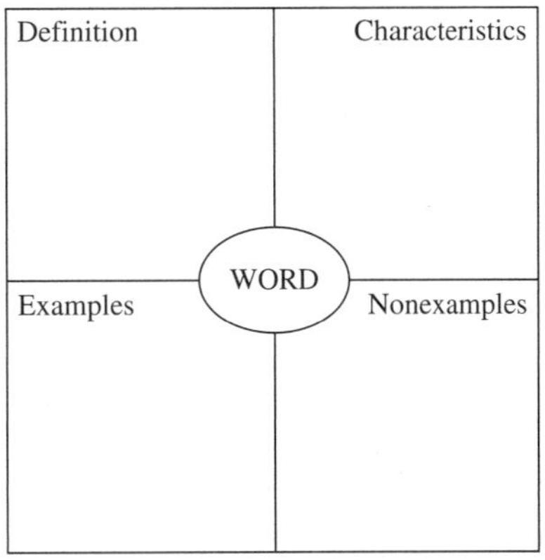

Learn More

Frayer, Dorothy A., Wayne C. Fredrick, and Herbert J. Klausmeier. *A Schema for Testing the Level of Concept Mastery.* Madison: Wisconsin Research and Development Center for Cognitive Learning, University of Wisconsin, 1969.

List-Group-Label

The List-Group-Label strategy offers a simple three-step process for students to organize a vocabulary list from a reading selection. This strategy stresses relationships between words and the critical thinking skills required to recognize these relationships. List-Group-Label challenges students to

- List key words (especially unclear and/or technical terms) from a reading selection.
- Group these words into logical categories based on shared features.
- Label the categories with clear descriptive titles.

Steps to Using List-Group-Label

1. Select a main topic or concept in a reading selection.
2. Have students list all words they think relate to this concept. Write student responses on the chalkboard. *Note:* Because the concept is presented without a specific context, many of the student suggestions will not reflect the meaning of the concept in the reading selection.

3. Divide the class into groups of three or four students. Have these teams join together related terms from the larger list. Have the teams provide "evidence" for this grouping—that is, require the students to articulate the common features or properties of the words they have grouped.
4. Ask the student groups to suggest a descriptive title or label for the collections of related terms. These labels should reflect the rationale behind collecting the terms in a group.
5. Have students read the text selection carefully and then review both the general list of terms and their collections of related terms. Students should eliminate terms or groups that do not match the concept's meaning in the context of the selection. New terms from the reading should be added, when appropriate. Terms should be "sharpened" and the groupings and their labels revised, when necessary.

Learn More

Taba, Hilda. *Teacher's Handbook for Elementary Social Studies.* Reading, MA: Addison-Wesley, 1967.

Lenski, Susan D., Mary Ann Wham, and Jerry L. Johns. *Reading and Learning Strategies for Middle and High School Students.* Dubuque, IA: Kendall/Hunt, 1999.

Semantic Webbing

Semantic Webbing builds a side-by-side graphical representation of students' knowledge and perspectives about the key themes of a reading selection before and after the reading experience. Semantic Webs achieve three goals:

- "Reviving" or "reactivating" students' prior knowledge and experience
- Helping students organize both their prior knowledge and new information confronted in reading
- Allowing students to discover relationships between their prior and new knowledge

Semantic Webbing takes two forms: divergent webbing and convergent webbing.

Steps to Divergent Webbing

1. Write a key word or phrase from a reading selection on the chalkboard.
2. Have students think of as many words as they know that relate to this key idea. Write these words to the side on the chalkboard.
3. Ask students to group these words into logical categories and label each category with a descriptive title.
4. Encourage students to discuss and debate the choice of category for each word. Write the students' conclusions (the categories and their component words) on the chalkboard.
5. Have the students read the text selection and repeat the process again. After reading, have students add new words and categories related to the key idea.

Steps to Convergent Webbing

1. Identify several themes in a reading selection. Write each theme at the top of a column on the chalkboard.
2. Ask students to share their prior knowledge of each of these themes. Write brief summary statements of this information beneath the appropriate category.
3. Encourage students to make predictions about how the text will handle the stated themes. Stress the context of the document (time frame, author's background, subject matter, and so on) as the criterion for making these predictions.
4. Discuss the predictions and have the class decide which are best. Write these predictions under the appropriate category on the chalkboard.
5. Have students read the selection. Record any new information (beyond prior knowledge) that students gained from reading.
6. Encourage the group to evaluate the accuracy of their predictions.
7. Require students to revise the information recorded on the chalkboard on the basis of their reading experience.

Learn More

Maddux, Cleborne D., D. LaMont Johnson, and Jerry. W. Willis. *Educational Computing: Learning with Tomorrow's Technologies.* Boston: Allyn and Bacon, 1997.

Stephens Vocabulary Elaboration Strategy (SVES)

The Stephens Vocabulary Elaboration Strategy (SVES) requires students to maintain a vocabulary notebook. Whenever the student confronts a new (or unclear) word, the student writes and defines the term in the vocabulary notebook. Students should regularly review these words with the ultimate goal of integrating them into their working vocabularies.

This strategy stresses dictionary skills. Students use a dictionary to define new words and their parts of speech. The dictionary also points out the multiple meanings of many words. Students use critical thinking skills to analyze the specific content of a reading selection to determine the most appropriate definition of a word.

Steps to Using the Stephens Vocabulary Elaboration Strategy (SVES)

1. Require students to obtain a spiral notebook to record new vocabulary words.
2. Ask students to write any new or unclear word in the notebook. Also ask them to write the context in which the word was used.

3. Require students to write dictionary definitions (including the parts of speech) next to any new word in their notebooks. For words with multiple definitions, students should select the most appropriate meaning for the context.
4. Encourage students to also define the terms using their own words and compare their thoughts with the dictionary definitions. Personal definitions should be revised to more precisely reflect the meaning conveyed in the dictionary, without sacrificing the individual's vocabulary.
5. Ask students to regularly review their growing vocabulary list. Encourage students to use these new words in their written and oral presentations.

Learn More

Brown, Jean E., Lela B. Phillips, and Elaine C. Stephens. *Towards Literacy: Theory and Applications for Teaching Writing in the Content Areas.* Belmont, CA: Wadsworth, 1993.

Word Sort

Often seen as word identification, vocabulary, and/or comprehension strategies, Word Sorts have been found useful in both elementary and secondary classrooms. In secondary classrooms, content-area teachers can use Word Sorts as both a pre- and post-reading strategy. Employing a pre-reading strategy, students can use their background knowledge to sort words and set a purpose for reading. Employing an after-reading strategy, students can reflect on what they learned and process their understandings of the text and concepts (Johns and Berglund, 2002). In elementary classrooms, word identification may be based more on word families, parts of speech, or common roots. In either situation, Word Sorts offer students a way to become more engaged in the words found in text and the world around them.

There are two types of Word Sorts: open and closed. Both can be adapted to content-area topics for math, social studies, science, and language arts (Vacca and Vacca, 1996).

Closed Word Sorts

In Closed Word Sorts, the teacher defines the process for categorizing the words. This requires students to engage in critical thinking as they examine sight vocabulary, corresponding concepts, or word structure.

Example

Categories (provided by teacher): metals, nonmetals

Words: nickel, bohrium, sulfur, mercury, bromine, lithium, krypton, cobalt

Student work sample:

Metals	Nonmetals
nickel	lithium
bohrium	bromine
mercury	krypton
cobalt	sulfur

Open Word Sorts

In Open Word Sorts, the students determine how to categorize the words, thereby becoming involved in an active manipulation of words. Whereas closed sorts reinforce and extend students' ability to classify words and concepts, open sorts can prompt divergent and inductive reasoning (Vacca and Vacca, 1996).

Example

Words: nickel, bohrium, sulfur, mercury, bromine, lithium, krypton, cobalt

Student work sample (categories chosen by student):

- Metals with luster and malleability
  - Nickel
  - Bohrium
  - Mercury
  - Cobalt
- Metals with high reactions
  - Lithium
- Noble gases
  - Krypton
- Nonmetals
  - Bromine
  - Sulfur

References

Johns, Jerry, and Roberta Berglund. *Fluency: Questions, Answers, Evidence-Based Strategies.* Dubuque, IA: Kendall Hunt, 2002.

Vacca, Richard T., and Jo Anne L. Vacca. *Content Area Reading*, 5th ed. New York: HarperCollins College Publishers, 1996.

Vocabulary Squares

Vocabulary Squares is a strategy best used with texts that are at or slightly above a student's Lexile measure, and it is an effective strategy in cases where the semantic dimension of a text may impede reading fluency. Vocabulary Squares consist of a four-part grid, each with a different label. Some sample labels include:

- Definition in your own words
- Synonyms
- Variations
- Part of speech
- Prefix/suffix/root
- Sketch
- Symbol

For each identified vocabulary word, the student fills in appropriate information in each section of the grid. This helps students deepen their understanding of key words necessary to aid comprehension or make meaning.

"Vocabulary Strategies" Anchor Chart (Starter Kit)

- Read words and phrases before and after the word for hints.
- Think about parts of the word that I already know (prefix, suffix, root).
- Think about what kind of word it is (noun, verb, adjective, and so on).
- Substitute another word that would make sense.

Additional Resources

Anchor Charts: Making Thinking Visible

Purpose

- Anchor charts build a culture of literacy in the classroom, as teachers and students make thinking visible by recording content, strategies, processes, cues, and guidelines during the learning process.
- Posting anchor charts keeps relevant and current learning accessible to students to remind them of prior learning and to enable them to make connections as new learning happens.
- Students refer to the charts and use them as tools as they answer questions, expand ideas, or contribute to discussions and problem solving in class.

Building Anchor Charts

- Teachers build anchor charts with students to capture strategies and key ideas.
- Students add ideas to an anchor chart as they apply new learning, discover interesting ideas, or develop useful strategies for problem solving or applying skills.
- Teachers and students add to anchor charts as they debrief student work time, recording important facts, useful strategies, steps in a process, or quality criteria.
- Students create anchor charts during small-group and independent work to share with the rest of the class.

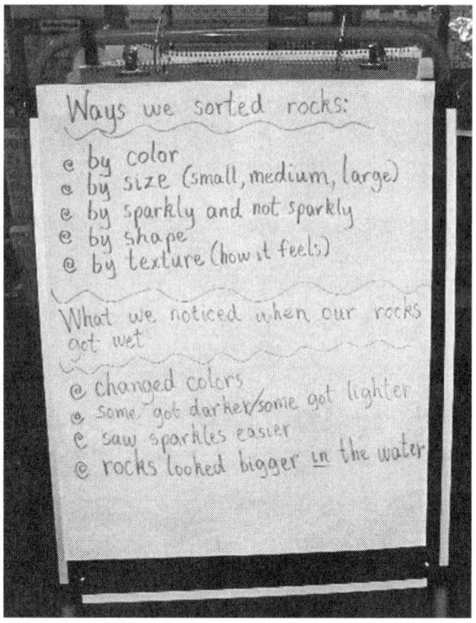

A Note on Quality

- Anchor charts contain only the most relevant or important information.
- Post only those charts that reflect current learning, and avoid distracting clutter. Hang charts on clotheslines, or set them up in distinct places of the room; rotate charts that are displayed, so as to reflect most useful content.
- Charts should be neat and organized, with simple icons and graphics to enhance their usefulness (avoid distracting, irrelevant details and stray marks).
- Organization should support ease of understanding and be accordingly varied based on purpose.
- Charts are best in simple darker earth tones that are easily visible (dark blue, dark green, purple, black, and brown—use lighter colors for accents only).

Annotating Text

Definition

Annotating text goes beyond underlining, highlighting, or making symbolic notations or codes on a given text. Annotation includes adding purposeful notes, key words and phrases, definitions, and connections tied to specific sections of text.

Purpose

Annotating text promotes student interest in reading and gives learners a focused purpose for writing. It supports readers' ability to clarify and synthesize ideas, pose relevant questions, and capture analytical thinking about text. Annotation also gives students a clear purpose for actively engaging with text and is driven by the goals or learning target(s) of the lesson.

Through the use of collaborative annotation (annotations made by multiple individuals on the same text), learners are given the opportunity to "eavesdrop on the insights of other readers" (Wolfe and Neuwirth, 2001). Both peers and instructors can provide feedback in order to call attention to additional key ideas and details. Annotating text causes readers to process information at a deeper level and increases their ability to recall information from the text. It helps learners comprehend difficult material and engage in what Probst (1988) describes as "dialogue with the text."

Procedure

1. Define the purpose for annotation based on learning target(s) and goals. Some examples include:
   - Locating evidence in support of a claim
   - Identifying the main idea and supporting details
   - Analyzing the validity of an argument or counterargument
   - Determining the author's purpose
   - Giving an opinion, reacting, or reflecting
   - Identifying character traits/motivations
   - Summarizing and synthesizing
   - Defining key vocabulary
   - Identifying patterns and repetitions
   - Making connections
   - Making predictions
2. Model how to annotate text:
   a. Select one paragraph of text from the reading. Highlight or underline key word(s) or phrase(s) related to the lesson's purpose, using the "think-aloud" strategy to share with students why you marked certain selections of the passage.
   b. Based on your think-aloud, model writing an annotation in the margin, whether above underlined words and phrases or to the side of the text.
3. Distribute the materials students will need, such as books, articles, highlighters, pencils, and so on.
4. Practice annotating with students, choosing another paragraph/section of text, reminding them of the purpose. Have them highlight, underline, or circle relevant words and phrases in the reading and add annotations. Have students share what they selected and explain the annotation each of them made. Repeat over several classes or as necessary, working on gradual release toward student independence.

References

Probst, Robert E. "Dialogue with a Text." *English Journal* 77, no. 1 (January 1988): 32–38.

Wolfe, Joanna L., and Christine M. Neuwirth. "From the Margins to the Center: The Future of Annotation." *Journal of Business and Technical Communication* 15, no. 3 (2001): 333–371.

Things Close Readers Do Anchor Chart (Starter Kit)

- Read the text slowly at least twice.
- Get the gist of what the text is about.
- Circle words you aren't sure of and try to figure them out.
- Reread, annotate, and underline key vocabulary.
- Use the text to answer questions.
- Gather evidence (quotes) from the text.
- Talk with each other about what you think the text means.
- Read the text again to summarize or answer specific questions.

Helping Students Read Closely

Determining the instructional sequence for close reading is based on three factors: the complexity and richness of the text to be read, the relative skill of the readers, and the tasks to be completed or understandings to be gained. Helping students grapple with complex text involves careful consideration of several factors and should be viewed as a series of decisions rather than as a rigid protocol. **The goal of this process is to develop students' ability to read rich, complex text independently and proficiently.**

Evaluating the Context

- Determine the purpose for reading. What will students understand or do with the information they acquire?
- Look ahead: Where is this heading? Why do students need this information? What is the assessment? What is the performance task?
- Choose compelling texts and/or be able to explain why a particular text was chosen: What makes it worth reading?

Analyzing the Text

- Evaluate the complexity (by quantitative and qualitative measures) of the text.
- Should students first hear a particularly critical and difficult passage read aloud? (If so, students need to follow along.) Or can students first "have a go" on their own and then hear the text read aloud after?
- What excerpts are particularly critical and difficult because of either complexity or importance that students will read them slowly, deeply, more than once, and with support?

- Attend to syntax and vocabulary. Determine what vocabulary students might be able to learn in context and what words will need to be defined in advance or after a first read.
- What essential parts at the start of the text, if not understood, will steer students in the wrong direction?

Launching the Text

- Students read chunks of text on their own, or you can read the chunks aloud (slowly, perhaps twice, with students following along to promote fluency).
- Students may need you to provide word meanings. Do this sparingly. Learning too many words before students read a text will overload students' working memory, whereas words introduced in context have more support.

Students Independently Making Meaning

- Students reread chunks of text on their own for gist. They think about what the text is about. Students make notes in the margins: What is this about?
- Support individual students as needed.

Clearing Up Misconceptions/Modeling

- Students discuss what they currently understand about the text as you listen in.
- Focus on key vocabulary.
- Note which academic words require more attention (based on how abstract the word is). Support students in determining word meanings from context clues and morphology.
- If necessary, define key vocabulary.
- Prompt for evidence and text-based responses through a well-crafted sequence of questions, probing in the following ways:
  - What does the text say?
  - What evidence do you have for that?
  - Is your evidence accurate? Relevant? Complete?
- Model only when needed, and only after students have had the first crack at the text. Use modeling as "mop-up."

Gathering Evidence from Text

- Introduce or reintroduce the purpose for reading and text-dependent questions.
- Students reread to answer questions (literal ones as well as those that involve inferring, synthesizing, analyzing, or evaluating).
- Students think about and discuss their answers in pairs or groups, focusing on details from the text.

- Students write answers to questions and/or share answers orally in response to your prompting (though writing is the best way to solidify and ensure understanding).
- Ultimately, students apply their learning from this text by selecting details as they complete research or writing tasks.

Closure

- Connect the work of the day to the purpose.
- Help students reflect on how well they are acquiring the expected knowledge and skills.

Meeting Students' Needs through Scaffolding

Lessons that involve highly complex text require a great deal of scaffolding. Many of the suggestions we make in the Meeting Students' Needs boxes are scaffolds—temporary instructional supports designed to help students successfully read texts that are supposedly too hard for them. Many scaffolds are excellent for all types of learners—English Language Learners (ELL students), students with special needs, and students who are just generally challenged by reading.

Scaffolding becomes differentiation when students access or have access to scaffolding only when needed. Scaffolds that are provided to the whole class might be appropriate and necessary, but whole-class scaffolds are not differentiation.

Front-End Scaffolding

Front-end scaffolding is defined as the actions teachers take to prepare students to better understand how to access complex text before they read it. Traditionally, front-end scaffolding has included information to build greater context for the text—front-loading vocabulary, summarizing the text, and/or making predictions about what is to be read. Close analytical reading requires that teachers greatly reduce the amount of front-end scaffolding, in order to offer students the opportunity to read independently and create meaning and questions first. Such reading also offers students the opportunity to own their own learning and build stamina.

The following are examples of front-end scaffolding that maintain the integrity of close reading lessons:

- Using learning targets to help students understand the purpose for the reading
- Providing visual cues to help students understand targets
- Identifying, bolding, and writing in the margins to define words that cannot be understood through the context of the text
- Chunking long readings into short passages (literally distributing sections on index cards, for example), so that students see only the section they need to tackle
- Reading the passage aloud before students read independently
- Providing an audio or video recording of a teacher read-aloud that students can access when needed (such as SchoolTube, podcasts, ezPDF, or GoodReader)

- Supplying a reading calendar at the beginning of longer-term reading assignments so that teachers in support roles (special needs, ELL, AIS) and families can plan for pacing
- Pre-highlighting text for some learners so that when they reread independently, they can focus on the essential information
- Eliminating the need for students to copy information—and if something is needed (such as a definition of vocabulary), providing it on the handout or other student materials

Back-End Scaffolding

Back-end scaffolding is defined as what teachers plan to do after students read complex text to help deepen understanding of the text. When teachers provide back-end scaffolds, they follow the Release-Catch-Release model, allowing students to grapple with hard text *first,* then helping students as needed.

Examples of back-end scaffolds include, but are not limited to

- Providing "hint cards" that help students get "unstuck" so that they can get the gist; these might be placed on the chalkboard tray, for example, and students take them only if they are super-stuck
- Encouraging/enabling students to annotate the text, or—if they can't write directly on the text—providing sticky notes or placing texts inside plastic sleeves (GoodReader is an app that allows students to mark up text on an iPad. Adobe Reader works on a wide variety of electronic platforms)
- Supplying sentence starters so that all students can participate in focused discussion
- Placing students in heterogeneous groups to discuss the text and answer text-dependent questions
- Providing task cards and anchor charts so that expectations are consistently available
- Highlighting key words in task directions
- Simplifying task directions and/or creating checklists from them so that students can self-monitor their progress
- Placing students in homogeneous groups and providing more specific, direct support to the students who need it most
- If special education teachers, teachers of ELL students, teaching assistants, and so on are pushed into the ELA block, teaching in "stations" so that students work in smaller groups
- Designing question sets that build in complexity and offer students multiple opportunities to explore the answers
- Having students discuss their answers with peers, then write answers independently and defend their answers to the whole class
- Providing time for students to draft-write responses before asking for oral responses
- Identifying and defining vocabulary that students struggled with
- Using CoBuild (plain language) dictionaries

- Providing partially completed or more structured graphic organizers to the students who need them
- Providing sentence or paragraph frames so that students can write about what they read
- *After* students have given it a shot: examining a model and having students compare their work to the model and then revise
- *After* students have given it a shot: providing a think-aloud about how you came to conclusions, and having students revise based on this additional analysis
- *After* students have given it a shot: reviewing text together as a class (using an interactive whiteboard or document camera) and highlighting the evidence

Examples of "Meeting Students' Needs" Notes from Lessons

Assessment

- Posting learning targets allows students to reference them throughout the lesson to check their understanding. Learning targets also provide a reminder to students and teachers about the intended learning behind a given lesson or activity.
- Discussing and clarifying the language of learning targets helps build academic vocabulary.
- Providing specific and focused feedback helps students set concrete goals for reaching learning targets.
- Developing self-assessment and reflection supports all learners, but research shows that it supports struggling learners most.
- Research shows that engaging students in the assessment process engages, supports, and holds students accountable for their learning. This practice helps all learners, but it supports struggling learners the most.

English Language Learners

Note: Many of these examples could be generalized to include "students who struggle."

- Consider providing nonlinguistic symbols (for example, two people talking for *discuss,* a pen for *record,* a magnifying glass for *details,* a lightbulb for *main idea*) to assist ELL students in making connections with vocabulary. These symbols can be used throughout the year. Specifically, these can be used in directions and learning targets.
- To further support ELL students, consider providing definitions of challenging vocabulary in students' home language. Resources such as Google Translate and bilingual translation dictionaries can assist with one-word translation.

- ELL students may be unfamiliar with more vocabulary words than are mentioned in this lesson. Check for comprehension of general words (for example, *law, peace*) that most students would know.
- For students needing additional supports and ELL students, consider providing smaller chunks of text, sometimes just a few sentences for a close read. Teachers can check in on students' thinking as they speak about their text.
- Consider partnering ELL students who speak the same home language when discussion of complex content is required. This can allow students to have more meaningful discussions and clarify points in their native language.

Protocols and Discussion

- Use of protocols (such as Back-to-Back and Face-to-Face) allows for total participation of students. It encourages critical thinking, collaboration, and social construction of knowledge. It also helps students practice their speaking and listening skills.
- Mixed-ability grouping of students for regular discussion and close reading exercises will provide a collaborative and supportive structure for reading complex texts and close reading of the text. Determine these groups ahead of time.

Complex Text/Close Reading/Vocabulary

- Hearing a complex text read slowly, fluently, and without interruption or explanation promotes fluency for students: They are hearing a strong reader read the text aloud with accuracy and expression, and are simultaneously looking at and thinking about the words on the printed page. Be sure to set clear expectations that students read along silently in their heads as you read the text aloud.
- For students who struggle with reading grade-level text, consider chunking the text for them on to separate sheets of paper. This makes the reading of complex texts more manageable and allows them to focus on one small section at a time.
- Text-dependent questions can only be answered by referring explicitly back to the text being read. This encourages students to reread the text for further analysis and allows for a deeper understanding.
- Some students may benefit from having access to "hint cards": small slips of paper or index cards that they turn over for hints about how or where to find the answers to text-dependent questions. For example, a hint card might say, "Check back in the third paragraph on page 7."
- Some students may benefit from having key sections pre-highlighted in their text. This will help them focus on small sections rather than requiring them to scan the whole text for answers.

Writing/Note Taking

- Consider having students who struggle with on-demand writing talk with a partner before they respond to the question in writing.
- Graphic organizers and recording forms engage students more actively and provide the necessary scaffolding that is especially critical for learners with lower levels of language proficiency and/or learning.
- Some students may benefit from receiving only section 1 of the text. This keeps them from being overwhelmed with the amount of text they will be working with.
- Providing models of expected work supports all learners, but especially supports challenged learners.
- Varying the methods of response for students makes the task accessible for all students. Offer students a choice to draw the things they notice instead of writing.

Additional Examples

- Guiding Questions provide motivation for student engagement in the topic, and give a purpose to reading a text closely.
- Anchor charts provide a visual cue to students about what to do when you ask them to work independently. They also serve as note-catchers when the class is co-constructing ideas.
- Adding visuals or graphics to anchor charts can aid students in remembering or understanding key ideas or directions.
- Many students will benefit from seeing questions posted on an interactive whiteboard or via a document camera, but reveal questions one at a time to keep students focused on the question at hand.
- Some students may benefit from being privately prompted before they are called on in a cold call. Although cold calling is a participation technique that necessitates random calling, it is important to set a supportive tone so that use of the cold call is a positive experience for all.

Rubric Basics

What Are Rubrics?

Rubrics are an assessment tool for communicating expectations of quality. They include the criteria that will be evaluated, describe various levels of quality, and are typically linked to learning targets. Rubrics are used to communicate about and assess complex products, performances, or process tasks. They provide a basis for self-assessment, reflection, peer assessment, and teacher assessment.

What Sets a Rubric Apart?

Rubrics are often confused with checklists, scoring guides, and criteria lists. The following are definitions that help clarify the differences between these tools.

Checklists generally include only the factors that will be evaluated. For example, a checklist may indicate that a product needs to exhibit originality, neatness, use of multiple sources, use of vocabulary words, and an illustration. Another example is a statement such as "Your product needs to include a thesis and three supporting pieces of evidence, five paragraphs, a chart, and a graph." A student could have checks in every box but still end up with a low-quality product because there is no description of quality.

Scoring guides include how each criterion is weighted—whether in points, percentages, or another measure. For example, a scoring guide based on percentages might indicate that Ideas are worth 50 percent, Organization, 30 percent, and Word Choice, 20 percent.

Criteria lists include both the criteria and a descriptor of proficiency—in other words, the "Accomplished" or "Proficient" section of a rubric. Criteria lists describe what factors matter and what they look like when done with quality. They don't spell out all the levels of quality; they just describe expected quality.

Rubrics include the criteria that will be evaluated and describe various levels of quality. The levels of quality are often labeled with the language of "Beginning," "Developing," "Accomplished," and "Exemplary" and associated with the numbers 1, 2, 3, and 4. Rubrics are typically more useful for students when assessing their own work, because they can match the work to the language of the rubric description and determine where their work falls in regard to each criterion. Rubrics give students language to describe the different levels of quality so that they can better describe their work and take incremental steps toward achieving quality.

Common Features of Rubrics

Rubrics can be created in a variety of forms and levels of complexity; however, they all contain three common features (Pickett and Dodge, 2001):

1. They focus on measuring one or more stated **learning targets** (content, skills, character, and/or craftsmanship).
2. They use a **range** to rate performance.
3. They contain specific performance characteristics arranged in levels indicating the **degree** to which a learning target has been met.

Advantages of Rubrics

Rubrics offer several advantages. Most important, many experts believe that rubrics improve students' end products/performances and therefore increase learning. When students receive rubrics beforehand, they understand what they will be assessed on and what level of quality is expected, allowing them to prepare accordingly and take ownership of their own learning. Additional advantages include the following:

- Rubrics improve student performance by clearly showing the student how his or her work will be evaluated and what is expected.
- Rubrics help students become better judges of the quality of their own work.
- Rubrics allow assessment to be more objective and consistent.
- Rubrics force teachers to clarify their criteria in specific terms.
- Rubrics reduce the amount of time teachers spend evaluating student work.
- Rubrics promote student awareness about the criteria to use in assessing peer performance.
- Rubrics provide useful feedback to the teacher regarding the effectiveness of the instruction.
- Rubrics provide students with more informative feedback about their strengths and areas in need of improvement.
- Rubrics accommodate heterogeneous classes by offering a range of quality levels.
- Rubrics are easy to use and easy to explain.

Creating and Using Rubrics

Here is a suggested seven-step method for creating and using rubrics (Goodrich, 1996):

1. Invite students to **analyze models of work** that range from strong to weak.
2. **Identify criteria** to be used in the rubric, allowing for discussion of what matters most.
3. **Articulate gradations of quality.** These categories should concisely describe the levels of quality (ranging from novice to expert or from beginning to exemplary) based on the range of work

samples. Using a conservative number of gradations keeps the rubric user-friendly while allowing for fluctuations that exist within an average range.

4. **Practice applying the rubric with models.** Students can test the rubrics on sample work provided by the teacher. This practice can build students' confidence by showing how the teacher would apply the rubric to his or her own work. It can also facilitate student/teacher agreement on the reliability of the rubric.
5. **Provide opportunities for self- and peer assessment** along the way.
6. **Revise the work** based on the feedback from self-assessment, peer assessment, and/or teacher assessment.
7. **Use the rubric for summative assessment.**

References

Goodrich, Heidi. "Understanding Rubrics." *Educational Leadership* 54, no. 4 (1996): 14–18.

Pickett, Nancy, and Bernie Dodge. "Rubrics for Web Lessons." *San Diego State University College of Education*. October 22, 2001.

GRAPHIC ORGANIZERS

What Do You See?

Observation	Knowledge	Interpretation
Describe exactly what you see in the photo. • What people and objects are shown? • How are they arranged? • What is the physical setting? • What other details can you see?	Summarize what you already know about the situation and time period shown, and the people and objects that appear.	Say what you conclude from what you see. • What's going on in the picture? • Who are the people, and what are they doing? • What might be the function of the objects? • What can we conclude about the time period?

Further Research: What questions has the photo raised?	What are some sources I can use to find answers?

Notices and Wonders

Notices	Wonders

Venn Diagram

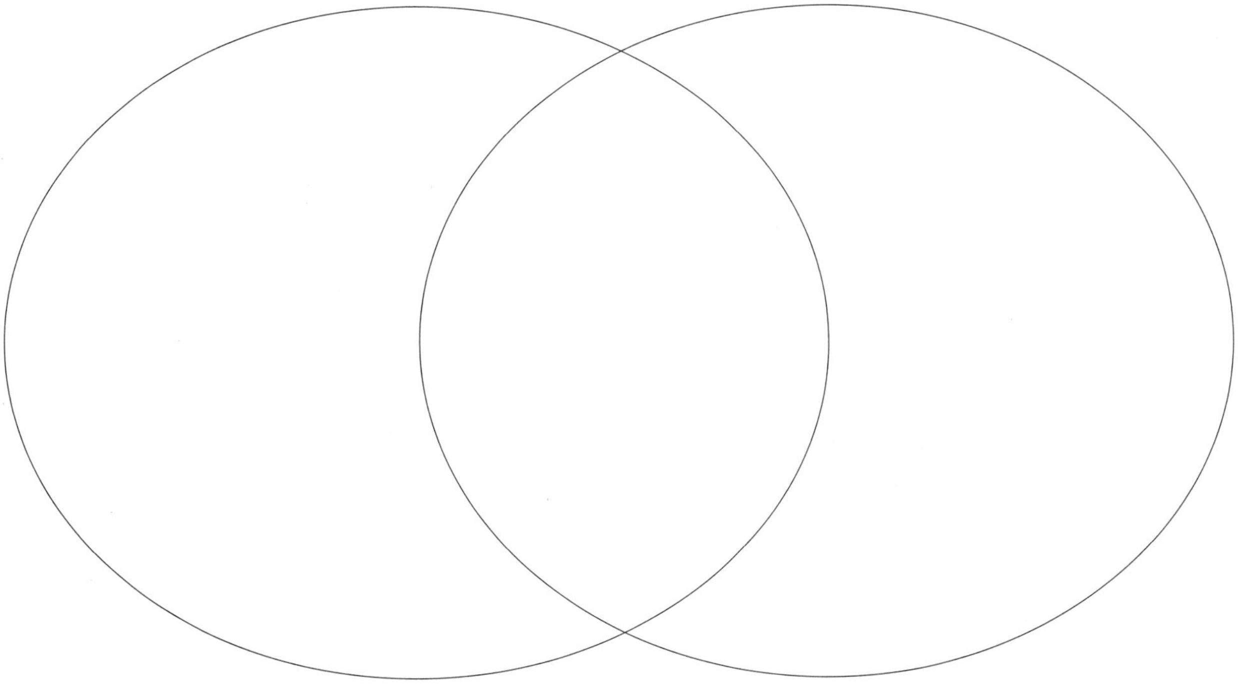

Jigsaw Recording Form

Name: ______________________________

Article Title: Presenter:	Main Ideas	Questions I Have
Article Title: Presenter:	Main Ideas	Questions I Have
Article Title: Presenter:	Main Ideas	Questions I Have
Article Title: Presenter:	Main ideas	Questions I Have
Article Title: Presenter:	Main Ideas	Questions I Have

Observe-Question-Infer

What do you OBSERVE?	What QUESTIONS do you have?	What INFERENCES can you make?

What? So What? Now What?

What?	So What?	Now What?

Four-Square Graphic Organizer

The first key idea/event: Details • • •	Another key idea/event: Details • • •
Another key idea/event: Details • • •	Conclusion

Topic Sentence

Learn More

Gould, Evan J., and Judith S. Gould. *Four-Square Writing Method: A Unique Approach to Teaching Basic Writing Skills.* Lancaster, CA: Teaching and Learning Company, 1999.

Paragraph-Writing Accordion Graphic Organizer

Topic:

Detail:

Explanation:

Detail:

Explanation:

Conclusion:

Topic Expansion Graphic Organizer

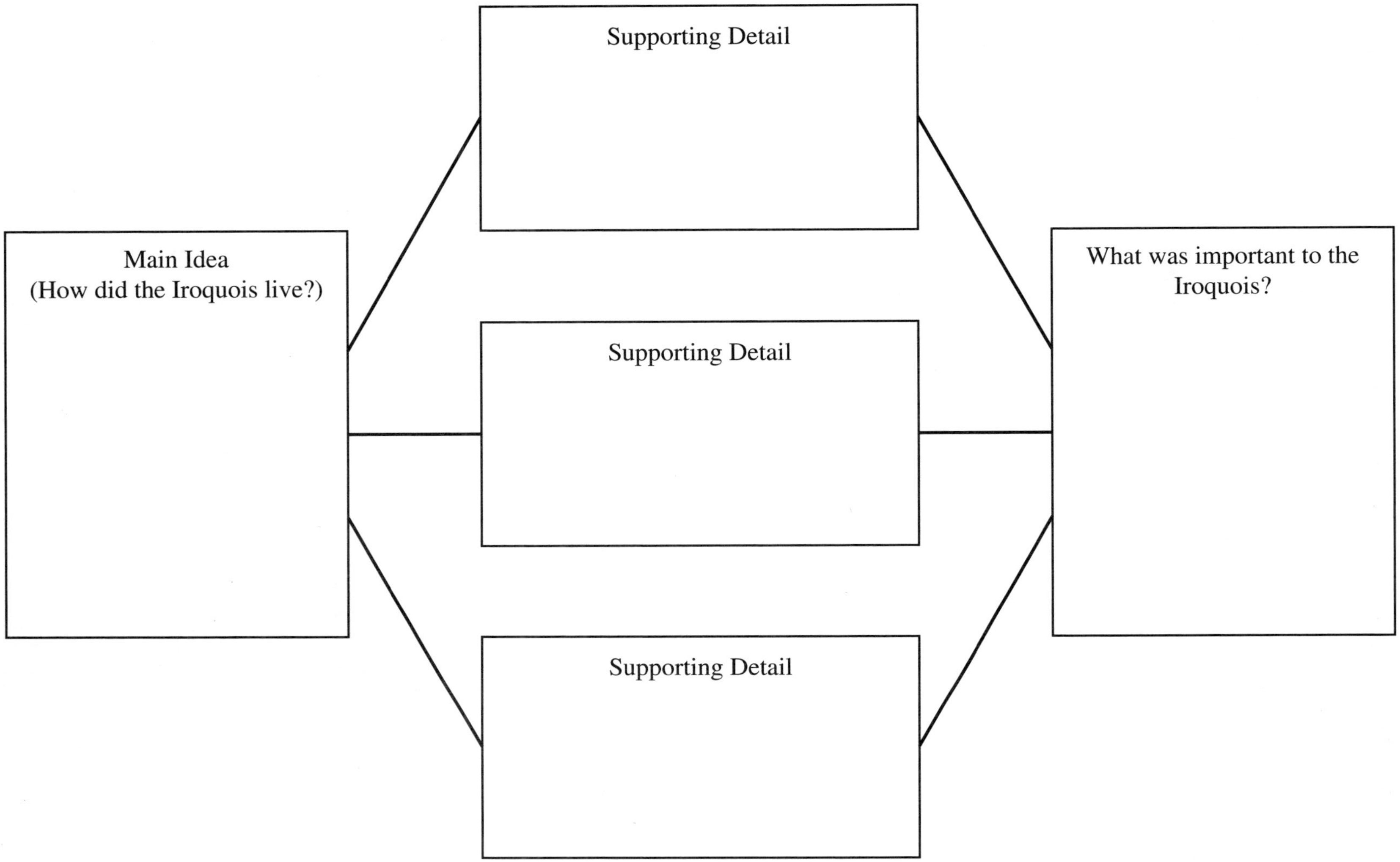

Building Background Knowledge Double-Entry Journal

Information from the Text	My Thinking about It Questions, connections, conclusions, and so on